penny kemp

binding twine

Book Design: Cape Traverse Associates
Typesetting: McCurdy Typesetting & Printing Limited
Printing: Les Editions Marquis Ltée

With thanks to the Canada Council for its support

Some of these poems have appeared in *Arc, B. C. Monthly, High
Hopes, Matrix, Origin, Arachne* and *Poetry Canada Review.*

Ragweed Press
Box 2023
Charlottetown, P. E. I.
C1A 7N7

Canadian Cataloguing in Publication Data

Kemp, Penny, 1944-
  Binding twine

Poems.
ISBN 0-920304-32-X

I. Title.

PS8571.E46B56 1984   C811.'54   C84-098671-8
PR9199.3.K45B56 1984

For the Mothers
For D. and L.

For Bill –
Cheers, and
thanks –

Pen
Nov 86

Other Books by Penny Kemp

Poetry

Bearing Down (Coach House Press)
Tranceform (Soft Press)
Clearing (B. C. Monthly)
Changing Place (Fiddlehead Press)
Toad Tales (White Pine Press)
Animus (Caitlin Press)
Eidolons (White Pine Press)
Some Talk Magic (Ergo Press)

Plays

Angel Makers (Playwrights Canada)
The Epic of Toad and Heron (Black Moss Press)
(reprinted by Playwrights Canada)
Eros Rising (produced by Theatre Passe Muraille)

Contents

At Stake

This is the testimony the judge did not, could not hear. From early 1974, when I separated from my husband, through 1980, our two children were in my custody. For four of those years I raised them on welfare. Child support payments were not met until a court order was issued. In December 1979 it was agreed that my son live with his father for a month. He stayed for eight months, seeing me daily. When he wanted to resume living with me, he was not allowed.

His father and the woman he lived with had decided to seek custody. Though I'd been glad to see my ex-husband take a more active role in parenting, I did not expect this. I wanted to avoid the strain of a custody trial, from which I could gain nothing—not even legal protection—since I already had full custody.

When all attempts at resolving the tensions failed, I took the children to Peru for four months. Our separation agreement had said the children and I could leave the country without their father's permission or knowledge. But I lived in physical fear of my ex-husband and knew that we would be tracked down anywhere in North America.

While we were gone, he got *ex parte* custody, which means that only his side was presented. I decided to return to Ontario to fight the case. I won interim custody in May 1980, though I was not allowed to leave the county. The children were allowed to see their father, but not the woman he lived with.

The custody trial took seven days over a three-month period in the summer. In December 1980, the decision was handed down. I lost custody.

My case was blatant in that the judge clearly condemned my values as outside the system. I had opted out of class, out of materialism. My political stance was one of voluntary simplicity. The judge shook his head and his finger at a nice, intelligent girl like me. Given all the advantages of upbringing and education, I had chosen to ignore society's goals. Worse, I was educating the children to be independent and self-sufficient from a young age. And I thought I was right.

The court decision confused me, undercut my confidence, any sense of security or belief in justice: another child of the sixties, radicalized without protective colouration. I thought I could be different, could offer the children a way of life free of middle-class pitfalls. I went too far and was caught up.

I am wary of a lurking desire for vengeance, a stridency. I am very aware of my fear of consequence. And I write anyway.

I have allowed myself to be victimized. I have learned. I do not allow myself to be victimized now. I take immediate action. I let nothing slip by. The central issue is passivity: how to break through the pattern of resignation, the sense of defeat and loss.

For years I lived in a state of shock, driven out of my body. Yes, my pelvis split at the birth of each child. Yes, I was beaten and had nowhere to go. The effect was I could not grasp reality easily. I saw things as if I were a foot above myself, hands at the ends of long poles, ineffectual. Now, having worked through the terror, I am here, present, willing to face what comes. Willing to let this book out in the hope that it reaches others who have been where I have.

One woman's account to every woman, every person. What *is* the role of society stepping in, telling us how and what to do, defining a good parent by a rigid set of standards? As if there could be just one *right* way. *Binding Twine* is about the "betrayal" by those women who saw me as breaching a code they had accepted. As a feminist, one of the more difficult things for me to face was the anger of other women who had committed themselves to patriarchal values. I bore the brunt of their attack without really understanding why.

It's my experience that most women going through such a trial think of themselves as utterly alone and indefinably "guilty," punished by the adversarial nature of the courts. It is those women I want to reach.

In *Binding Twine*, I speak to people who might not normally read poetry, though in times of such stress they might write. Poetry is to me the natural medium for highly charged and conflicting emotions, dealing as it does with the complexity of life. I'd like to make the leap to poetry possible for more readers.

In my experience, poetry is a kind of sympathetic magic. I believe that if I can articulate a situation exactly in the writing, then the original problem will take a different form. The writing will reflect back into my life as a gift of awareness. It might be a very primitive sort of thinking, but it works for me.

My task has been to transmute my personal experience into something larger, more accessible: to make my truth available, so that a correspondence is set up with the reader. I don't know why the run-on lines of prose are considered more accessible than poetry. Poetry can say so much in a single phrase. A tuning of the ear. A response so that the words matter. It has taken three years to muster the objectivity and courage to write this book.

For me, the writing carries one through the process of victimization into a new active stance of clarity and understanding. I want to thank all those friends and loved ones who agonized their way through with me. I am grateful to Louise Chisholm, Cathy Ford, Honor Griffith, Carole Itter, Anne Kemp, Joy Kogawa, Don MacKay, Suniti Namjoshi, Sharon Thesen and Phyllis Webb for their close readings of the text. Special thanks to Libby Oughton, midwife to this book.

Penny Kemp,
Mattawa, Ontario
February 2, 1984

Given the First Seven Years

Changing Hour

The mothers are blind, the fathers are lame.
They stroll holding each other's hands.
Haltingly. Halting to admire wild flowers.

The fathers are blind, the mothers are lame.
Knowing no boundary, they take what is not
theirs. They give what is not wanted.

They have crept round the hill.
They have not returned. How
are the children to learn?

Mothers, fathers, brothers, lovers
gone into the fog of
gone, gone in the fog.

Sisters, children, animals, birds
glum in the damp green dusk.

Left bereft, the children,
sweet lights go out.

When We Could Be in Flight

We are all children who have left
the mother and leave the father be-
hind. We phase out our first life
without rite, without rights
to initiate new. Wide-eyed
we are borne aloft before we
are willing to be born. Chrysalis
cracks. Wings ripped.

The years we mourn, we spend at-
tempting to mend those wings.

The Law of Sevens

What comes in sevens? The
phases we know. Snow White
was princess till seven, then
shocked into a forest octave,
till she was ready
at fourteen to know her
work: to be Queen. So I tell

my children who are impressed
with being seven! the weight
and roundness of cells, one
cycle complete.

At five times their age
I contemplate the changing series
in the divine chaos we live.

The number seven will split us,
opening the door to the world.

But they, my dears, starting all
over again, whistle away as we
do the round of beds and plates,
one for every dwarf and each of us.

The Great Mother

Our daughters cry out to us
as if we were mothers. Our
mothers cry out to us as if
we were daughters and mothers.

We can't answer till we know
we are mother and mothered.

Somewhere behind cerebral cortex
rests another mother.

Remember to become night sky,
tending her store of stars.

Take care. Take care away.
My daughter is lonesome. I
can't be there till I'm be-
yond the great divide, human
and divine, that lies between us.

Mother daughter motheraughter
mother ought. And then there
are fathers. And sons.

September Light

"I like to rush today," yells
Jake. "I got five minutes to
do everything I want before—"

laughing his way out the door,
leaping between seasons as
juncos swoop pine in return.

The morning's alight with all
the vigour of reprieve. Wind
and sun sweep the haze clear.

After a fast bike ride, a fast
lunch (peanut butter, lettuce and
mayonnaise), the receptive rests.

Could we stay in that place, a
light grace for both of us? First
day of school, new pencils, new
books and hope. Don't be late!

Ready or Not You Must be Caught

Are you ready? Get ready. Now.

I'll be ready when nothing
sets us off, tops spinning
higher and higher pitched.

You'll be ready to drop
your voice out of whine.

Don't miss the boat.
Don't miss the bus.

You'll be ready when you leap
out of Batman and Robin to
make the bed you dream on.

I'll be ready to move
my hands through clay,
flour and soft folds of
seams you help guide.

We'll be ready when this is
done and this and this and...

It's almost too late. It's
never too late. Let's go!

Jake Recounts His Dream

There once was a boy named Ziekel
and he was an Indian. His sungods
were angry at him because they didn't
like him. So he was angry at them.
He ran away from his mother and his
family. His mother tried to find him
but he was farfar away and nobody
could find him. Then a pigeon came
and a parrot. They said, "What are you
doing here?" He said, "I'm lost and
my family is lost too." The parrot
asked, "Do you like bananas?" "Do you?"
"Yes, I do." "Do you like the feathers
I'm giving you?" "What feathers?" asked
Ziekel. "My feathers," said the parrot.

His family was really worried now.
A hawk came to Ziekel and said, "I
want to eat you up." But Ziekel ran
and the parrot and pigeon lifted him
on their bright wings. His family was
so worried now. But Ziekel was flying
till the hawk got tired. Then an air-
craft came and scared the hawk. It was
night now. Flying by, they saw all the
planets in the night sky.

The sun had gone, the sungods too.
And nobody knew where they were.

Son Gone

Mis / Take

"A boy needs a father," they said.
I believed. When he asked, I thought it
only fair. It seemed right.

Even though I wanted him to know
a woman's peace in himself, I
let him go. Young. I gave him away. Now
I pray he can hold his own. There.

Holidays

By this word
I let you go
to your father's world.

By this word
remember
while you are there.

By this word
I won't ask you back
before you are ready.

By this word
I sever the silver blue cord
taut between us.

By this word
be eight and out
exploring.

By this world
hi and goodbye
and see you around.

Passive Tense

I knew and I gave my son anyway.
I knew where my son was going.
I knew whom I was giving him to.
The rage. The violent frustration.
The power turned in upon itself.
The tenderness hid in bristle.

And still somehow I thought he
would survive intact and come back
at the end of his holiday.

We agreed on a month. But one
stretched on into many.

At least now his father
sees him. Isn't that
what I asked for?

This Time It Is, As Well

Once it was war
that took the sons away.
Or disease, famine,
unsanitary conditions.
Boarding schools. Convention.
Anything other than our
volition.

Now it is liberation.
Or the courts.

About Face

I tried to think like a man.
I followed reason, reasonably.

He knew where he was going, or
thought he did. I let him go
against my instinct and my will.

He caught my confusion. His father,
backed by society, had none...
Maybe he needed to learn other values.
I assumed a mother was not enough for
a boy to grow into a man, as surveys
of single women raising sons showed.

I thought wrong.

Pragmatics

"I've got money now," he
grins, rattling loose
change, flipping dimes
in careful succession.

Computers and video,
his intent. High tech
prosperity. He designs
secret spacecraft to save
the planet from pollution.

Child of the eighties, he
plans to ask for military
aid to get the rocket up.

He boasts. He brags.
But he doesn't deny
by veiling his eye
what together we knew.

Isaac's Story

What seems to be our undoing
is the binding of the son
in sacrifice.
              No last minute
panic. No hesitation. He
does not balk.

After that terrible
surrender, the hiatus
in time might last a
month, a year, an aeon.

Who knows its reverberation?
Our degree of trust determines.

As soon, as surely as we agree
to offering, he is raised
from the altar we have built.

The bond is the boy's
release. The cutting
of the bond is ours.

The twine unties us both,
apart and laughing over
the last barriers.

Allowances

Our sons who choose
the ways of the father
embrace the world as
they leap off our laps.

Sallies out of home base.
They go where they know
the learning is now.
Our imprint received.

We raise them so far,
then set them loose
for a breathing space.

Open Air

Trust the boy's need to
escape powerful wings,
ducking out from under
to try out his own.

Let him fly into the net
coincidence sets shaking
of his own sweet schemes.

Deliver him from archetype
I spread as mother.
Shadows beat against the pane.

Women Spirit

Patterns

Giving and giving as women
were taught by generations
of mothers. Giving out of
nothing. That is something
only the goddess can expect
to continue forever.

Once we denied our daughters
to feed our sons, as if
their importance was inherent.

Now our work is with girls.
And women.

Just Us

"There is one in the spirit,"
sings Amanda and her heart
is in the right place at
the right time. With mine.

"Let's the girls be together.
And the boys be together.
Then we be private."

If we would live open to this
there is family: you and me.
Let us sing together. At last
you have my full attention.

Powerful Maiden, second child.
What happens to you concerns
us both. Delighted. Determined.
I feel it.

Dream (Mind Your Wake)

Amanda's walking on
the smooth and murky lagoon.

She pokes under lilypads
humming her new song:

"There's a world in the frog
and a world in the womb.

There's a world in you
and a world all around.

You are all the world!
You are everything!"

"NOT POSSIBLE!"
A neighbour startles her,
glares alarm alongside.

Amanda falls in, is
righteously fished out
on the hook of the long red pole.

The neighbour lady hands her
sopping to me for safer keeping.

"When I Was Little"

Who's afraid of their shadow?
I used to be. I thought it
was a ghost coming after me.
I was scared of myself. Now

I creep along beside me and
do everything I do. At noon
I grab myself and shake me up.

   Little one, alone, I am
always with you.

My Mother Warns

Daughter, do not answer
the faint cry—the one
you almost hear
through trailing vine.

The mutter of the far-off
bird, of the rotten
tree: ignore.

Let it ring vaguely
out there.

Let me persuade you.
Your hair is always so
curly. Do not listen.
Do not respond.

Such calls bring the
beyond
too close.

We are farther
than ever from our
fathers. He is gone.

And you will die if you
listen. We all will.

Nonetheless

That depends, the dream insists.
I push, push away the mothers'
voice inside my head.

I will hear for myself. Awake.
I whistle to my daughter, join
me. Look at that. Listen.
Can you hear the low call?
Piping staccato, persistent.

Other voices. Other choices.
Come with me. She'd rather
later, when her friends are out.

How long before I notice
no one can tell
my mother's voice from mine.
Gentle and fiercely low.

My daughter's voice has not yet changed.
Maybe she will surprise us.

Sequence

i

Amanda is falling   falling
falling   from the parapet,
from the sweet certainty
she posed for, poised
on the edge like that.

So many storeys down. So
many stories. Each ledge
she could choose to stop
her for a life time. Her
life line now spins taut.

When a neighbour phones
to tell us she is dead,
she is dead, Amanda herself
answers the call.
Disconcerted, she passes
the message to me
through my anxious mother.

Looking both ways, I see
her whispering here
and spread-eagled below.
I hear her tell the tale
as though it was happening
as she was telling.

"Double the double," she
mutters. "What's going on
around here?"

Talking and falling, or
recalling falling

ii

No time to tell her to
hold on, no time
to teach her to fly.

Thought cannot hold
a double reality
any more than
my arms can reach
the little girl
on her way down.

That trouble behind her,
she is keen to practise
to perfect her
balancing act.
Ropes and spikes, tricks
of the trade.

The look on her face
contains her flight.

After All the Looking

She returns on her own.
We weren't there where she was.
We were home where she wanted
to be all along, she says.

"Did you say grace already?"

The circles concern are still
spinning. She includes the slack
by taking up arms.

"Believe me believe me you gotta
believe me!"

The white hum of fear
constant at back brain
shifts to reverse as
we look it, as we look
her in the earnest little face.

"I believe you all the time.
Especially when I don't lie."

Tension, This Cling

The spine taut
on a hanger
holds to its own
neurosis as if by
osmosis.
Bones stiffen.

Vertabrae frozen in line
like cold clothes
waiting some chinook
out of the west
to fan sheets in the wind
of a possibility

I've lived along—
a sliding scale of
corresponding emotions.

Pleasure and
duty like laundry
that wanted doing.

And on the face,
an echo of those same
lines, too many for
twenty-nine or thirty-
five, etched about
    the eyes, the mouth.

One Way Out

Thaw

Over and over
an hour
a day, a life,
devote
this task.
Sit. Still.

Kids come and go.

What is to be done
here where
the waiting
has been
waiting for.

The valley
fills.
Drops collect and merge,
collect and fall.

Only the fingers type:
small whirling stars

fall into the well
and over.

Bidding Spell

By Saturday cleanup.
By Sunday love feast.
By goodnight cuddles
        come back.

By your new bunk bed.
By rocketship plans.
By acting the hobbit
        come back.

By chinese checkers.
By your skill at chess.
By the lost game of Probe
        come back.

By skates. By skis.
By blue hockey cap
        come back.

By your moon in Capricorn.
By your Gemini rising.
By your sun in Leo
        come back.

By your shining face.
By your amazing inventions.
By your magic tricks
        come back.

By your folly.
By your fairness.
By your ancient soul
        come back.

By our sweet bond.
By the space we accord.
By the spirit we share
        come back.

By Aslan. By Superman.
By Gandalf. Come back
when you can.

Check-Up

I took my son to the dentist,
I told his father first.

When she saw us return,
she pushed me aside:
"Don't you dare take him
anywhere. You have no
right. He is mine now."

In that moment, I chose.
We left the next week.
He had no cavities.

Interiors

There are no ceilings
to these poems. Doors
are walls. Windows
look out. Look out.
The floor. Floored.

These poems are without
landscape, without setting.
The season is usually
winter. The time
completion.

The absolute of cold.
Snow and nightfall. Time
to ponder. No compromise
between extremes. No exit.
But out the door. South.

The poems are cords of
dialogue, slack and
taut, taught and vocal.

Do Not Pass Go

The worry.
The hurry.
Arrangements
fall into place.
Out of place.

Correspondence
school.
Correspond with them
later. From a phone
booth, on our way.

Out of harm's, at arms'
length. At arms.

No choice but to
go. Nothing furthers
but flight.

Shh. Can you come?
All the way to
Peru. And back.

He will relent.
He did before and
before that.

(I forget
to figure on
her.)

The Last Time

His hands closed on my neck.
The cord once again tightened.

I flew out of body, a white
bird pealing, drifting
out of bounds.

The kids kept me
hovering close,
on the edge.

Now nothing
stops me. Not even
his reprisal.

Her Mind Set

Snake: You are the only person
        in the world. So I have
        to bite you, good Food.

Only Person: How about you bite
        yourself?

Snake: Oh, I can't. It would
        kill me. I'm so long.
        I'm so thin. That's why.

Only person: Well, you can't eat
        me! I'm my own food.

Snake (sobbing): Oh, please! I
        haven't eaten anybody
        for two hundred years.

Only person: When first I came here
        we were friends. Now look.

Snake: Gobblegobble. Yum yum.

Only person: Yikes! I'm getting
        outa here. Help! Good thing
        Snake gots no legs.

So she ran and she ran until she came
to a valley where was an apple tree.

And she could eat apples all day long
and no one could bother her there.

"How I Spent Christmas"

We speak Spanish now.
We write stories in English.
We ride in many buses,
some of them new, some old.
We stay in many houses,
some made of mud, some fancy.

We live on the Island of the Sun.
Llamas, alpacas and burros.
Chickens and pigs and sheep.
I'm going to be a shepherd,
like my friend who is ten.
One day a condor came real
close. We climbed way high.
You wouldn't believe so
many different things we see.

I only missed one thing:
Christmas. But we had one
here too. Popcorn in soup.
Things we can give away
those children will like.
One for you, one for you.
And muñecas burning away
the Old Year. Happy New!

Swimming Hole

Surfacing, surfacing, the fish
jump and nibble. A kingfisher
stoops and squawks off empty
above the dam we piled high
with rocks and branches.

We swim in the cold water.
The mottled stones are still
sharp, enlarged and rounded in
water. Wind rippling. Light.
Laughter louder over water.

Too many black flies speck
the sight. How can I escape
a sticky web of little fingers?
Footsteps over dry leaves.

Your father reels me through
you to his intent. Sound all
bassoons: *Peter and the Wolf.*
Splash away past ghosts.
Family name, given names.
Let's bake mudpies in the sun.

Ex Parte

Furies, you chase us across
the continent. We are passed
hand to hand, laughing like
coyotes from the penthouse.

Know that we chose to run, to
return to your home ground
though we could have disappeared
for years. Running was always
within our power. And our rights.

At Stake

The Trial

Seven days over
the whole summer.
Thirteen witnesses for
and against.

The worst thing about
the system is it's not
funny.

Humour more or less
undone in defense.

In court I grinned
at some inanity
and was reprimanded.

Not to make faces.
Levity. Gravity.
Lips are pulled down.

Subtle digs I dug:
the kids called
unkempt, my name
undone.

It did not occur to me
to lose.

The Whole Truth

Dirty laundry. Unmentionables
piling out of every closet.

I did not tell the whole truth
on my lawyer's advice, for fear
of jeopardizing my position.

The pelvis I split when pregnant
kept me periodically flat
on my back. I couldn't carry.
Their father agreed to ferry
the laundry to a laundrymat
as his contribution.
When he reneged I washed
our clothes in the tub at home.

Preparation

The boy dreams he dives down
the laundry chute and is burnt
in the incinerator. But God,
even-tempered, revives him.

We circle round and round a
life-long widening spiral,
attempting to articulate
what we trusted at four and
forgot at eleven. What was

lost in that flood, we can
just glean from the mess.

Jake dreams he's in a land of
zombies but does them all in.
I know he's fine. He can leave.

All in the Wash

Drips from the drying clothes,
snow sizzling on the fire.
Before we know, we have already
known.

My laundry is less white
than white though I too use
Tide. I guess I swim against.

Clothes revolve around a
spindle in swirls of grey.
Never clean enough. Maybe
they're packed too tight.

Something to do with filling.
We fill and are emptied.
We can choose what and where
to pour. I choose to return

the waters of love to the living
earth. Dirty water. Clothes
scrubbed, scrubbed till the cloth
wears out.

      The way of fire would be
neater.

Reading "The Raw and the Cooked"

Do you want to see fire?
I'll pull the string of
my rocket car.

That's fire. Sparks.
Makes not hot but GO!

Do you want to see my golden Eggs?
Ten in a basket: play dough.

Do you want them to become one?
First squish. Then rub.
Then roll. All one.

Do you like this?
Do you like this?

Not so hard and not too soft.
Not well done. Just right.
Like so.

Do you want to see fire?
Another fire makes hot.

One & one & one & one.

The Dreams Multiply

In the last few days before
the children find out where
they're bound, I wonder aloud
for them: What would you do, if—?

We'd write; we'd say just what
is happening. "Oh, so that's
what a letter is. I never knew."

Mail me drawings and stories
so I may know where you are,
reading between the lines.
The sweet lies I can trace
of invisible ink.

Subtle ways we conjure to cross
space. Memories and songs from
the middle brain act as refrain
for you to repeat. There are
methods. This is conditioning.

Remember me. Remember what is
of value. I had so much yet to give.

Christmas Eve

I have known for a week now
and told no one. That night
the judge in my dream said No.
That was the first indication.

I woke up, heart pounding,
stretched beyond itself.
That day the judge decided.

I cannot believe it. I won-
der what to do. I wanted
to have a good Christmas.

All night I lie convinced:
this is a heart attack. My
chest is ripped apart, heart
exploding. In the morning
after we open stockings,
I enter Emergency alone.

The cartilage is torn from
the bone. Round and round
they bind my chest. My heart
contracts in its cavity again.

Mom's annoyed I am sulking.
So I tell her what's happened.
And my father and brother.

Running and Laughing

The kids are laughing
in another room with
their little cousins.

Run again. I could.
Run again. I'm not
going to.

Laughing in another
room. I want them
sealed for a little
while longer from
what Christmas will
reveal.

Soon enough. Laughing
in another house.

The Last Presents

Christmas afternoon. The presents
have been handed round.
We have gorged, we have sung.
The treasure hunt is over.

Powder snow on hickory limbs,
spreading tree I climbed as
child, clinging to in need.

I have something to tell the children.
We reach the tree through snowfields,
chatting of anything else. Let's
talk about Peru. No, let's talk
about the sparkle on the ice crust.

Blue sky, deep snow and we lean
together against the broad trunk.
Children's eyes, blue in white faces.
Their rosy cheeks. Their curious
hearts. This our last present.

Care and Custom

They know their father's coming
to get them. But not for how long.
Children, we have lost the court case.

Tears lie like crystals in his
widening eyes. "Well, mom, I guess
that's the way the cookie crumbles."

She melts against me mutely. "Oh mom
you didn't. How could you?" Only I
notice her slight shift in person.

We walk back hand in hand.
The car is already waiting.

She's seen enough movies to
know her lines off by heart:

"You mean now is the time
that we must say farewell?"

No Appeal

"Why bother? Not a chance.
They will only appeal
your appeal. And on and
on it will go until you
are run into the ground.

Think of the children.
Wait and see how it goes.
Tossed back and forth.
Wait and see how it goes."

Oh lawyer, it has gone.
They have gone. All for
the sake of our principles.

Replays bring us no closer
to what did happen. Moral
collusion, slander, chance,
fate, poor planning, blithe
ignorance: all or none or
some of the above. I don't know.

I do know you feel bad. Too bad.

Truth or Consequence

Once he let me choose:
"Do you want to be my wife
or do you want to write?"
I chose.

Overdue payments.
Windswept pavements.
Black ice.

When the kids were small
he and his support were gone.
Seven years I raised them.

Now the hard part is over
he appears to take them.
Responsibly.

The Bride

Fourteen years ago.
I should have known.
Nobody told me
I wasn't supposed to
really try and
cut the ceremonial
layer of cake.

The wedding party waited,
smiling, smiling,
for the toasts to go on.
He tried to help.

Blood dripped from my finger
on waves of white linen.

Testimony

In his testimony he never
never spoke against me. He said
I was a good and loving mother.
For that I forgave him a lot.

She and their lawyer were furious.
I assumed the case was over then.

When they won, he drove the streets
for three days in his cab. Crying.

Reflective Poems

The poems deal less with him
than with shadows, reactions,
reflections, her, them,
the mothers.

Why? Why not tackle
society, the patriarchy
head-on?

      Because poems
don't take the place of
action   and action
failed.

Marthas and Mary

His mother loved me
though she didn't know me.
But I was too snotty by
half. Who did I think I
was, not to do a wife's
work for her son?

So she believed the lies
told by someone she did
understand. Together
they blow implacable,
steady, fierce and cold.

The Gift

So you want to suck my marrow
and strew my bones about
the neighbourhood.

Who says you are dark?
My bones collect themselves
into a new order.

Feed off me as you will,
I am not there.

Take the man I ran from.
Take the house I discard.
Take that life. It is no
longer mine.

I shed a skin for you,
the one I grew out of.

Coming of Age

I write poems that give
her the power of evil
intent. Intent upon
analysis I give away
my power of action to

her, an ordinary kid,
anxious to please. From
the age of fourteen, living
with the man I married.

Now she is twenty-one
going on forty, starting
her third cycle. Suddenly,
she wants to mother kids
she had ignored for years.

When she decides to hate
me, her ulcer disappears
and the kids can be hers.

She is happy in her choice.
She is happy in her chosen
family. All she wanted
was a home. And a family.

That's why she fights so hard
for mine.

Appointed

The court decision I could justify.
The judge was old and wanted peace.
He slept through the proceedings.
He knew their lawyer well and mine
was on his first case, out of town.

The stories their witnesses told on
the stand I could laugh at, sure
the judge would hear as well as I
their contradictions. I dismissed
the details that were their case.

(The red snowsuit Amanda adored
I let her wear with ripped knee.
"The kids were left to wander late".
"The kids were kept in after supper.")

The court decision I could almost
accept, for a while. The children
understood how hard and long
I'd worked and I was tired. They
would have money and new things.

We could just enjoy each other
two weekends a month, a day in
town and half of the holidays. She
would soon weary of constant child-
care and gladly return them home.

Sorting, For the New Wife

I shower upon you the detritus
of childhood. Half-broken toys,
games with one part missing,
clothes a little too large
that will do soon enough. All
the cards, mementos, drawings
none of us could have discarded.

You can. Empty green garbage bags.
Choose, sort. Select. It is what
you do best. Be careful what to
throw out. And what to keep.

The children have chosen what to
take. They know what they want.

So Help Me God

I thought a court of law
was a court of justice. That
truth would be seen to be
truth and lies to be lies.

So while she went about
persuading witnesses
to testify, I stayed aloof.

The truth, the truth.

But the ladies whom I passed
on the street with a smile
to get home to write:

The ladies believed her.
The judge believed her
and her shrewd lady lawyer.

Blood Mother

The Banana Eating Competition

I sang with the children
in different languages.
Whenever I travelled,
they came with me.

We always came back
to our little blue house
with the rainbow gable
and the inside swing.

My children were not allowed
sugar or meat or much TV
even at other people's homes.

My arrogance was such
I didn't care what
anyone thought. I was
not about to concern
myself with pettiness.

When neighbourhood kids
came to play I gave them
the time I never had for
their mothers. In the end
I was the one not allowed.

Such a close community
if you obeyed the rules
of Home and School.

I was a bad mother
to ignore the code and
stupid to think I could.

Witness Stands

The Montessori school asked us
to let the children walk home
independent. I did. You said
I let my children wander back.

Your kids run around shit-
caked and snotty-nosed,
bare-assed in November. You
claim my kids are slovenly.

You say you couldn't reach me
when you phoned for the kids.
It's true. We had no phone then.

Your boy abuses my daughter.
You call it my carelessness:
at two she could have said no.

Your boy is deemed "disturbed."
I talk to him, he talks to me
when he can tell you nothing.

Why do you testify to your own
short-comings, the ones
you see as mine?

Teach me what you mean by
what you say.

Fancy That, A Shame

"She can't just fly off without
a word like that. Who does she
think she is? I took a look at
one of her books, makes no sense."

"Did you see what she's wearing?"

The mothers aim arrows
to ground me. No kites
allowed. They want me
tied to apron strings
like theirs, ready to
role play. No chance
of change. Aloud.

"Well, she can't get away with it."

Opinions handed out over coffee
till I swell like them, stymied.
I called her, I called her, a fat slob.

The First Stone

Liar, liar, pants on fire!

Nothing you say can
harm me. Nothing you think
to convince those who thought
they were my friends.

Who among you would not have
evidence equally slanted
against you? Consider it
slander. Consider it.

Sticks and stones.
Brittle bones.

Letters of the law.

I read the children
too many fairy tales—
You call me a witch.

What is at stake here?

The Charge

The mothers are hounding me.
Bitches, they drag my scent
to earth and buy me deodorant.

They rant, they wring hands.
They blacken their mouths
with fire-fierce chants.

Ladybugladybug, fly away home.
Your house is on fire and
your children will burn.

Protect your own, mad mothers.
Circle round, babes to centre.
Small grey elephants trumpet
amok, stampeding: oh maenads,
where do you run to? Why
run me down? What in me so
scares you?

Hand Me Down

The mothers are betrayed
into upholding traditions
that keep them in place.

The ritual rape of daughters
that mothers perpetuate.

And the daughters return
of their own accord.

Betrayed by the voice
in their head. The mother
speaks. The daughter

mouths the words as
her own. Compliant.

Where are the sisters who know
what they say to themselves,
to each other.

I am surrounded by
mothers.

Hollow. Hello.

The Setting

Changing, I am changing, the lady
whose smile disappeared in tiger's
maw. And the tigers circle round
a tree, change to ghee. No change
of heart. Aw gee, what did you
expect? Tigers and elephants.
Hyenas watch and laughing howl.

The mothers are barking up the wrong tree.
The mothers have wrung me limb to limb.
The mothers have clung to my breaking
bough. Down will come baby, cradle and all.

All for a change of clothes.

We Are Tigers

We are tigers
what bite!
what bite my mom.
I have no mom.
They ate my mom.

We are tigers
whoooooooooooooooooo
what live inside the mountain.

That is the end of the story.
That is the end of the story.
That is the end.

Now the ghost part.
That's going to be mine.
shhooooOOOOOooooooo.

Don't be scared.
Ghosts aren't real people.

We are wonderful sight.
I think I could ride down this rope.
We are GIANTS! And we eat
tigers.

I think I could speak to the giants.
Hello, hello?

In Place of Persephone

Here I hide in darkness,
sullenly squeezing red
pomegranate seeds.
The bright sky shut my eyes.

There was a field of flowers,
viper's bugloss, blue and red.
Their pink buds brighten crimson,
violet and then deep blue.

Sometime I will return.
Not now. Too much hurt
reverberates the will.

The mothers still curse me with sharp
insatiable teeth, hissing through gaps.
His mother. Hers. Her. And likely yours.
The generations swell enraged.

I chew the pomegranate slowly.
No gaps in my teeth. Here I am
young. I am beautiful. Eating
this fruit I am almost inviolate.

I am the unfading flower.
I disappear half a year.
They seek me out. Close.
I am in. Closer. Closet.

Mothering Instinct

The power grows in me.
The will to be different
from them. To effect
change.

I become what I'm called.
I am a witch. Howling.
Rampant the she-bear.
The white sow squealing.

Rage prances, it dances
with jabs neat and sharp.

I don't know for how long
before the red bull roars.

The sweet surge rises,
floods till it's over.

Alfalfa sprouts, mung
I swallow alive, chew
the potent green juice.

Power spent, futile.
Ineffectual. In effect.

Ranting in the wrong ears.

Blood Ties

I am as happy as rage
uttering these curses
between clenched teeth,
careful not to direct
words too closely so
as to cause bodily
harm. I wouldn't want
that. I wouldn't want

vengeance on such a
nice day. Sun shines
on frozen bay. Even
the wind has abated.

Last night I danced to
the full moon, bright
through clear icicles
guarding my porch, a
row of jagged teeth.

I let moonlight bless,
caress my huge belly,
swelling not with a
birth but old shit
and menstrual blood.

The Dogs

I will not let them through the door.
I will not let them in.
They are tousling white kittens.
They are dousing the geese in the pond.

Last night she stalked into my house,
fur coat clutched black to her chest.

She asked for my children.
She asked for their things.
She asked for the table
on which sat my typewriter.

She got the children.
She got their things.
She got more writing
than she could have dreamt up.

I kept the table and
the typewriter.

Evil, evil, evil, I mutter
wild at the sight of the teeth
she clasps her cloak by:
white plastic rows between red
grinning lips. A buckled lip

I shut the door on. Shut your
eyes and shut your mouth.

The dogs are nibbling at my heels.
I will not feed them any more.

Untimely Ripped

Out / Come

Face to face the void.
Avoid the façade.

I can't stand. It.
Not yet. Where there's
a will. A way. Away.

Am I willing to have this mean
what it means to you out there
reading? What is in. Is all.

The rage. Tend. Tender.
Enrage. Outrage. Wrath.
Wrong. Wrap. Wild. While.
Wile. Kill. Kill flies.
Time flies. Kill time.
Watch. End the night. Wait.

Weight. Whine. Want. Out.
Better me out. Butter me up.
Out is not in. What is in is
all the rage. What does it serve?

Late Night Poem

I would like to sleep for weeks.
I can't sleep a night through
since they left. What more,
what else might be taken?

After the earthquake, the fire
the revolution, the treefall, I
slept as sound as the children
sleep now. Sleep now. Has been
taken too.

Making up for all past blindness,
eyelids, violet eyelids will not
close. Limbs akimbo stiffen.

How to sleep. How to wake UP.
I need to see, I need to sleep.

Happening. What was (is), I
did not escape the shock.

Pain, pain, go away. Come again
some other way.
Not this. Not this. Weary.
Wary. Worry. War. Were. Worn.
Out.

Fairy Tale

Pass this way again.
Not likely. Age
and the times do
not bear children.

But witness.

Passing fancies.
Over lightly.
Once. Upon.
Court. Hearing.

Passage, rights of.
Unheard.
Passage, nights of.
Heard. Said.

A time. Bear in mind.
To come to my truth
will I reach yours?
Here. Hear. It is.

Un / Mother

For most it is gradual.
For some it is not.
How do I act with out?

Without that wake I
drift. Unmoored. Not
yet unmasked. But

unasked, the barrage
of questions I need
no longer attend.

Unanswered. Space
surrounds. The ghosts.

Who am I then with/
out them. Who. When.

Longing

All along something, sometimes
in the chaos of diapers or box
lunches, wanted out. Now that
same restless It wants back.

It clings to my self-image.
It clings to my attachment.
It clings to my position as
righteously it feeds off lies
and deception, discontent.

It forgets the lovely irony:
Yes, you can have everything
you need. But not necessarily
at the same time. Nor when
you decide you want it.

Strings

I wondered what it was like.
I'd never lived by myself.
I'd never slept in a house
alone. Instead I'd slipped
from family into marriage
the day after graduation.

I thought I was independent.
Nonetheless.

Shadows

Because of the atom bomb
I figured at twelve that
only thought might last:
the transfer of a mind
onto the page. Shadows
on Hiroshima walls.

I had children, thinking
ten years of life better
than not knowing at all.
But that was the most I
could conceive for them.

Ironic how our pledges
turn to haunt us, living
out their own reality.
Each child taken by ten.
The work remains: turning
the page. Such subtle twists.

Words on a Page

Words on a page
you are not likely to see.

I don't know why I should feel
guilty. I feel guilty.

Free to do as I like like this.

I didn't expect it to be this
hard, now that I am free,
only to be free.

Un / Mothered

Who has been towing
whom? I thought I
was your source. But
you were also mine.

I no longer tell tales
at bedtime.

On the street, I am no
longer safe.

The Medium

Children, you no longer hear me.
Children, you no longer see me.

I am a voice without a tongue.
A talking head with no eye.
A phone that rings no answer.

No answers.

Children, you no longer know me.
I no longer know you.
Children, you no longer need me.
I need you.

In Different Modes

Long Distance

i

She had to go.
She really had to go now.
Because she was told.

She was colouring
inside the lines
of a flower design,
she forgot the name.

Watching a re-run
and about to eat supper—
spaghetti and wieners, what
she liked best now,
when I called.

So she really had to go.
Sorry.

Situation. Comedy.

ii

Outside the lines, loss re-runs
bad breath between us.
In the background, canned
laughter blows its lid.

Applause mounts revolt.
For that which is is not
as it might have been.

My belly turns in on itself, claws
its cave empty, gnaws a way out.

iii

See you, see you. Soon.
The black cord connecting us curls
taut. We hang up. Over and
out. Hanged for a. Hung up.

The cord of the receiver
attacks my guts, pulling out
a mess of spaghetti and wieners.
It looks like the junk I was
damned for not serving the kids.
Splattered in floral designs.

iv

The cord turns umbilical blue
and snaps. The flower she coloured
violet and pink vibrates off the page
into my heart's black hole.

Cherubic fingers part the skin
to let the light spread,
a violet and pink transplant.

The cord that was electric blue
shrivels and blackens. I bury
umbilicus under the lilac bush.

Sooner than anyone ever expected,
she had to go. She really had to go.

Impasse

You try me. You test
every nerve. You wish
I were dead, disappeared.

How do I keep faith?
I say you are doing
fine by the kids.
"Better than fine,"
you reply. I say
I don't even dislike you.
I hate what you've done.
How can you believe me?
"Bullshit!" you snort.

I whose work is with
women am stymied. How
can I maintain?

Invisible Shield

You gloat over your ap/
parent win. Now live
with the knowledge of
what you have taken.

You are very young and
old beyond cold eyes.

I don't wish you ill
but I am waiting. You
think I am gone and you
are right. But know
that I do not intend
ever to disappear from
the lives it was mine
to bear, to bring forth.

Hang Up

Do you not realize how
your hate infects the kids?
So to live in your house
they have to disrespect
both my values and me?

"You aren't even worth hating."

Don't you know the kids
will pick that attitude up?

"Are you telling me what to
  feel? I can't hide that
  and I won't to please you.
  The kids know. And besides
  their father keeps telling
  them how much he despises you."
Click.

"In My Mind"

Conversation
could be worse,
turning and turning on
the same theme. But I
doubt it.

When are you coming?
"I don't know."
When will you know?
"I don't know."

(The voice, muffled,
reminding the child of other
commitments.)

Do you love her more
than your own mother?
"I don't know.... No."
Please tell me you love me.
"Can't I just say it
        in my mind?"

(She is listening.)

When will my gut learn
not to churn. Admit
it, admit it. I hate.

To Each Her Own

Shadows and projections. We've
woven demons round each other.
Well, I withdraw and leave you
to your own. Alone with them.

They remember everything and they
are watching. This is no curse
but a blessing, of sorts. Though
there can be no escaping my
presence. Sometimes you will see
me through their eyes. You will
hear echoes of my voice in theirs.

Sometimes you will not know which
is which.

At Odds

For all the mothers
confronting other
mothers, mirrors to
their own shadow.

How do we confront
what we cannot see
hidden in ourselves?

She is everything
I am not. I am
what she can't be.

We can never get
even. We can't
even admit what
we lack or despise
is the other in us.

Thin. Short. Fat. Tall.
The children claim
we're about the same
weight and height.

Laughing, I multiply.

Inches, between.

Stepping Out

How do we step out
of this arms race?
Disarming me does not
disarm her. But what
more can she do? Dead
or alive, I threaten.

For years I tried
returning her hate
with what I called
love, superior.
That gave her hate
body. Now I send

indifference, so we
don't waste more time.
I step out of the game.
I choose another.

Face to Face

Visitation Rights

I write poems.
I speak out.
Power returns.
Body unknots.

But what's a word
in court of law?
What's legal aid
against his money?

The terms are fair.
They are not met.
What's a decree
against the fact:

the kids are there
and I am here. Every
other weekend I wait
for them to come.

I said nothing for fear
of not seeing them at
all. I complied, I

compromised, I let
them break their
commitments to come.

What I did did not
matter. They came or
not. I have nothing
more to lose. So I

write this book for
you who are also
alone, without a word.

Safe Bet

I pledged if I lost the case
I would write like mad.
If I won, I would not.

When I lost I could not.
Until I wrote myself
out of dissolution,
disillusionment,
toward my own
authority.

A solution I claim
to move on.

The Gain

The loss is not
that I chose to create
this mess. I accept
that set-up somehow
though I might have
managed it better.

The loss is recurring
upset. Once is never
enough in the process
of letting go. Again.

The loss is never
growing around fear
or grief or rage.

The gain is a web
woven around empty.

The gain contains.
Mother and child. No
way but through loss.

The pattern closes on
the hole of that loss.

Finally

What is there left to mother but
my own despair, my own unquiet body?

Who else for me to comfort?
Who else to comfort me?

Only the full embrace of
loss will bind me. Empty
armed. But tighter now
than any other love.

Nothing but loss could show me.
Nothing but loss complete me.

For giving. Forgiving.

Power Plays

I admit manipulation,
rigidity, pride.
Received assumptions
of right action.

I act as if I still
controlled the children.
I do not.

Telling them
what to do, when.
They don't have to.

I lose the face
of my own authority.
I who never did
what I was told.

I wheedle, sulk,
coerce, blame, try
to persuade.

The tyrant in me
is tireless but
unconvincing.

I lose face.

What choice is there
now but a rough
humility, a ruthless
contemplation of
events.

After Loose Ends

For all the mothers
in the thick of things
who let an era end
when it is time.

For attending that time,
its need and variation.
The fullsome, the fresh
equinox harvest, entry
into the sacred half.
The falling silence.

For the mothers so soon
free to grieve, knowing
the house is waiting.

For the empty well-made
beds, the spoiling food.
For the toys disappeared,
the floor quickly swept.

For the mothers who bide
the time suddenly theirs
when all is in order. All.

What I Didn't Take Into Account

Things the children needed or
wanted. Things I thought I (we)
could do just as well without.

A poverty of things I liked.
I lacked. Some things. No
thing. Just enough heat if
we gathered driftwood for fires.

Just enough food to last
from what I had preserved
till the end of the month.

Always enough second-hand
clothes, some of them quite
nice, I thought. Never any
extras, but who needed extras?

I liked a poverty of things.
I bound my children to be
poor of necessity. And of
choice. We always got by.

We were always so much richer
than they (brown faces)(black).
What right had we to more?
No right but the kids' desire.

The Mothers of Peru

Remember those other mothers,
those whose children disappeared
under the sea, in earthquakes,
in prison camps and uprisings.

Those whose babies are dying
too starved or sick to cry.
Remember their question, their
plea, and what could I do?

The river water ran typhoid
but was delivered by truck
and most mothers bottle-fed
encouraged by plump ads.

Remember their resignation.
The terrible passivity that
might have been acceptance
if they weren't so tired.

Remember those children dead
of diseases mine shrugged off.
Measles. A fever. Coughing.

Those are my children too.

Picture my own, playing and
squabbling, safe. And be glad
for them.

Generation Gaps

So I can wait out the years
before you return to show me
who you are, what you can do.

I give up needing you
before you come back.

You know where I am and how
to get here. It would not
matter if I were closer.
Home is the boundary we chose.

Already I am obsolete, betting
on the past like that, when
nothing then prepares for now.

I write you stories of great-
grandmothers and their antics
for you to tell your children.

Your attention is the present.
I know you must choose to be
where you live. To forget for
now. I am here.

Passing

Idling in the passage of kids,
the present is lost between
memories and predictions.
Whom do they take after? What
will they become? We forget
the space that dropped out
in the presence of children.

We thought we were twenty.
We wake up forty. Worn
with the weight of unlived
years. One morning we are
mothers. By noon we are not.

The time it takes to turn
to other things.

Survival Games

The Buffers

I'd write poems
from the kids' view
point if I could.
If only I could.

Worlds in collision.
No rules of conduct.
Adult entrenchment.
Terrain with no maps.

You seem to be fine
in the buffer zone.
You walk carefully
between the camps.

You do what you want
most of the time. I
worry how it is for you,

turning one world off
for another at whim.
Too much power so young.
Though you try to be fair.

I wonder how you will
survive without scars.
Hiding unhurt in neutral.
Not that you don't care.

But that you can't be seen
to by the wrong side.

Continuum

You know what missing is.
A face, a grin, a touch.
The catch at the throat.
Memories on the mindfilm.

"I didn't live with dad.
Now I don't live with you.
But my brother's been with me
all my life. Isn't that
something?"

We could breathe in again
those projections we so
easily exhaled at the
heart's murmur.

"Life is hard," I declared
at five to my mother.

Meanwhile the present,
when we are ready to
forgo the old loops
and pull in the slack
to our own heart's core.

"And Then What Happened?"

That link of pictures past
the children half recall
but hold me fast to.
Connecting their line
back to source.

Photos and stories.
Beginnings. Reminders
of this other history.

Leafing through the pages,
they paste in extras, can't
wait to fill one scrapbook
and start the next.

Looking Forward

Weekends return us to
family, easily complete:
till the hour crossover.
Too rapid goodbyes.

Another world leapt to
before they have left
the joy that a family
affords. Too soon.

Too late. What if is
dead. Long live what
is. Let them tell me.

They catch their life
on the run, not looking
over one shoulder
understanding backward.

Coming Home

I make ready for sudden
changes of mood, theirs
or mine. For tiny betrayals
that otherwise snowball.

If I reckon with after-image,
subtle shifts of affection.
If I melt away jealousy.

If I can cut through a thin
overlay of new ice among us.
If I thaw the shards and
splinters I let pierce.

If I can remember the right
song at just the right time.
If I lay in enough juice,
ask over the right friends
and stock up on spaghetti:

Then we'll pretend that all
is as it gently was. We'll
return to the common pool
of love, swim and bask and
have a good weekend.

The Changes

At first the children found
the changes fun.

But then. They preferred
not to come. "Just going
through a phase,"
my mother would say.

I can't pull the cords
that used to connect us.
The power is not hooked up.

"It's enough just to see you,
mom," he says. "As soon as
we're with you, it's just
the same as ever. You will
never change. You're you."

Living through the swirl,
I don't understand him
until I visit my mother.
Of course she's just the same.

Remedies

I studied homeopathy.
I foraged wild foods.
We drank herbal teas.
The kids were seldom ill.

Now they are eating normally.
They get colds like everyone else
and take their medicine righteously.
As they need to. All the same.
All the same.

With Me You Were Special

It was all too easy for me
to give the mundane away.
I don't miss video baseball,
lost mitts, complaints over toast.

I let you go into other hands
to rear you till you are
normal. Or ordinary.

In the words of my mother,
"Never saw off." Where is
the humility to let you
choose your lives fully
regardless, with blessing?
So you can bloom uncompelled.

The secret redeems us: what
else is there to bind us?
I let you be.

Meeting My Weird

My fate slips away
from the hands of
the children, just
out of reach. Out
of hearing.
Hands off.

"Weird," she calls me
offhand, and ears
are turned.

Do not dismiss me
so lightly.

Do not pretend my love
is not. It is.

Sure. Be happy.
And. But.
Remember.

Win. Lose. A fate
beyond control,
it seems. It happens.
And who or what
creates the outcome
is not within
my grasp.

The Fair

The grappling claw
grabs mechanically,
quite at random,
for the trinket
in the bowl of prizes.

The grappling hand
articulates more
than I can.

The simple solution:
Win. Lose. Yes. No.
Approval. Dismissal.
And winner take all.
"Who said life was fair?"
parrot the children,
running off with the gilded charm.

The Camps

The children are learning
about power, willfulness,
lies. Lying works and is
seen to work, it wins.

Two truths are told.
Each teller is right
and thinks s/he is.
Each honestly thinks
she is being honest.
Each righteously
claims she is right.
The other is lying.

The children are learning
how to manipulate. How
to be fair. How to lie.
How to know their own truth.

People say, "Oh the poor
children caught in the middle!"
But they've worked it out
to their advantage.
They have it both ways.

Lies at Play

The web you call your tricks
twists in about you till you
consist of what you invent.

Words twin their own company.
You forget your first intent.

I watch your eyes to understand
your mouth. The ears tingle.

Your illusion is clear.
Its necessity is not.

I prepare new ways of knowing.
But what can I tell you until
you are there and back again?

Sleight of hand, having it
both ways, little trickster.

What will you become, my
master tactician?

Persuasion

Generous and
benign savours.
Pumpkin pie pleases
the nostrils of
children and gods,
drawing them near.

How does she do it?
The plans, the presents,
Promises, kept or not.
It doesn't work when I try.

"The difference between you,"
Jake tells me seriously,
"She makes dad think
that he decides. She lets
him talk and does what she
wants. You didn't let him
believe he has the power."

Will we never mature into
true nurturing? Learning
happy endings as if they
were still possible.

The Claim

What do we do with our
power that sees itself
as love? And in reaching
encircles, ensnares us
both in boundless moebius
strips. No buffeting edge.

Where power is, there is
no love. Think about
Solomon's tale: the true
mother would rather give
over her child than have
him split in two.

"Your heart is big enough
now to let go," announces
the dream voice.

Take power away. What's
left is choice to love.

Mother, the Name I Reclaim

Upstream

Lifted out of our element,
the daily round of things
to be done and for whom,
I cannot breathe the sharp
space that might be freedom.

I gape after the active
emptiness the children
fan. The bright spectrum
they desire spins them away.

I who remember their long
spawning can not now still
that frantic swirl. Caught
unawares. Astonished.

Till I recall in their wake
what by bucking the tide
I denied.

Complicity

We have been fish
in a net of light
swimming cross-current.

We are also the net.
We chose our design
as it seems to happen.

We know also it is this
our children have chosen.
A web's small intricacy.
The play of sun on water.

What we do not know is
why. What will reveal
the total pattern? When?

Fish fall to pieces in
the stream where they spawn.

The net holds. But what
will contain the net?
We scry so little, under
water.

Personal Effects

It happened. It happens.
All that happens to me
seems to reflect my intent
whether I know it or not.

I watch how I choose.
I know my intent by (in)
(through) what I do.

So we adapt and evolve,
learning what it means,
the effects of each act
which we thought isolate.

Evolve, turning out from
under. Spiralling
on.

Down the Line

With our backs turned,
how can we see both ways?
Our mothers' needs, our
children's, our own.

Turning point.

We look for love from them
who look for love. We send
what we call love to those
who are swaddled inward,

turning. The layers our
love sinks through, sinks
down to reach our hope.
Connection. Be there please.

The distance we span as
buffer deceives us. Back
to back, the long line of

women, looking ahead to
what they were and behind
to what they will become.

Our heads spin on their pivots.

Transmission

It's taking too long.
One or both of us will die.

Her fear is mine.
I breach, I panic, I
turn around right
in the dark red passage.

This is the terror
we pass on to
our children
who lie shivering
forever.

The cord that fed me
I feel the rest of my life.
Wrapped round
my neck. Cut off.

Is this how intelligence
starts? Regretting.
Regressing. Redressing.
Requesting.

The Second of February

This is the day a mother
may reclaim her daughter
lost to the underworld
these many months since
we mourned our girlhood.

This is the day the daughter
returns, retracing slow steps
up the steep path home.

Flowers await her, the feast.
The great year turns a new cycle.
Elements shift and seasons,
the fierce embrace of poppies.

But why does the young one
fall slack in the open arms,
why is the purified one
empty of essence, what has
possessed her, my daughter?

Shadows on the thick snow, a
black dog romping like fear,
like memory, and the poppies
turn poinsettia.

Relatives

I'd like to get to the truths
of this. All is not well.
We stoop to conquer.

I speak. You speak. Do we
listen? Thank you for
demanding I hear you.

The truth is. The truth is
I have not liked you well enough.
The truth is how absolutely
I do love you.

Two truths are known. You. Me.
Same. Similar. Not other.
I did not want to be you.

I did not want to like you
when you wanted me to be like
what you wanted me to be.

Two truths will make us one.
The truce shall set us free.

High Hopes

What can I say as you too
at eight enter the world?
Your friends curl their hair,
wonder what on earth to wear.

Your colours blend, you know
all the rules of camouflage.
You're becoming your friends
and I am not their mothers.

Practise looking pretty just
like your friends and their
mothers. Blow dry your hair
and brush the sheen round.

It's so straight and you hate
it, so pin it up. Roll it.
Make it just like the photos.
Nothing different. Wear a new

cranberry dress and cranberry
shoes. There's so much to lose
it's hard not to choose with
the others. And their mothers.

When you're eight. When you're
late. And the world is waiting
for you to catch it by a braid
and swing it round to a bun.

Till your friends watch what you
wear and copy-cat how. Beauty,
you're such a big girl now.

Easy Answers

Cutting through space, a vapour trail
your movement follows you. You think
the moon in the water follows you.

The moon image dances the thaw
among chittering ice floes as
you shake your head to the song
inside. The two of you shining,
dancing rainbows through the fog.

"Want to see the moon sing me
her very own song? Want to
see the moon move after me?
She'll do anything I want.
One, two, three, four. Go!"

There are more illusions to this
game of beauty than you can count.
Or count upon. Catching cold.

For who can say but you wherever
the sun gathers sundogs, refraction
of its bright intent. You are sure
you are the sun, you are the moon.

One among many. And only you know
what's true in the shimmer of desire.
So many guises to beguile you into
the chill of glamour. So young.

Well, Well

Mothers and Daughters

Our daughters push beyond us,
when the power is strong,
unrolling the future to
certainty.

We can no longer stand
behind our rules. We have
only our word and theirs
to be free. All we can do
is learn without
obligation. To. From.

I free you free me.
Liberation intertwined
with a difference.
The cycle of generation
spirals once more.

We return to our mothers,
offering them the gift
our daughters offer us.

How It Was

I loosen the cord that
binds us tight in knots
of nots, lots of loss.

Somewhere the kids are still
laughing, loyal, poking
elbows into ribs, creating
versions of a story for
nostalgia.

Was it like that?
It was like that.

I am tying up loose ends.
I am binding twine.

The Twine

These cords that bind
the kids grow out of.

The false stories we tell ourselves.
The children are growing. Up.
Out of. For sure.

If they were with me these three
years. I would not have written
this book. Might not have written
period.

What will it do for them, reading,
I can see them, so carefully.
I'm careful to be as fair
as I can stretch.

I wish their stepmother would
read the book and hear, for/
give, let up.
I know their father could,
he was always a good reader.
But might not. Be able.

The false stories we tell ourselves,
the slack cord of hope.

Exercise

A field of flowers, bright red,
and blue sky, wind rippling...

You come in stretching, ready
in green and yellow leotards.

I no longer wait for the myth.
I enter the unfolding story
for a pattern that will hold.

Uphold, withhold, hold in
and you too shall be thin.
Taut belly taught not to
breathe. How we push up,
sit up, fit and physical,
to reach the next rung.

Panting to articulate what
the flush of dance enhanced.
Breathe in. Breath out. Belly
swells, falls. Field, flowers
find other poems. Let it in,
oxygen. To keep up with you.
The secret is in the long breath
out.

The Link

"I look like my dad
on the outside.
but on the inside,
my mind's like yours."

Our keen ability
to guess each other's
thoughts and feeling
serves us now.

Before you sleep,
see me sitting by you.
Hear me singing and
join in. Let me come
in dream and rock you.

For nothing, no one
can interfere
unless we allow.

An Abstract for Events

My thought is in my body.
Carry it on. My thought

is my body, carrying on.
This is a woman speaking.

No. This is a woman as
she is. Speaking. After you.

Cleft

For those who are called
to carry through acts
they trust but don't
understand. For those who
recognize a river antlered,
a new course taken.

For the way from state
to state, stage to stage
ellipsed in a moment.

For those who are suddenly
there, prepared only to
surrender what we hold

most dear. For the love
that cleaves us to do
what we must and when. As

the word "cleave" means
split apart/cling together.
The pun speaks its layers

the moment we listen to
the integuments of love
unwrapped, unmuffled.

The Facial

Mother, I take your hand
and thank you, whom I so
long resisted, running
backward in a panic to
be more, other than an
ordinary mother. Just
as you taught me.

I fought the flow of
your order to maintain
my separate space.

I danced askance off
your anxious image, twisting
to be deflected.
I never dared look direct.

Now I see in your face
what may be my own.
Behind the lines, eyes
connect light restraint.

I wash off our masks and
laugh as you begin to
laugh. I dance in your
traces   and on.

Make It Glow

For those mothers who remain
ashore and shoring, mending
the holes, cutting the cords,
gathering stray strands.

Weave the common thread
wide and strong. Make it hold.

Make it glow like that
first cord we almost
remember, the one they
cut off too soon.

Well

For the mothers
who spot the pattern
and laugh
          laughter
digs wells in
the dried clay
our tears made moist.

We are jars that love
has filled   emptied
   and fills again.